The Royal Princes
William & Henry

compiled by
AUDREY DALY

Ladybird Books Loughborough

Prince Charles being congratulated on the birth of his son William

Crowds at the hospital

The Palace announcement,
21st July 1982

Erratum: Page 4

The Palace announcement,
21st June 1982

Acknowledgments:
The author and publishers wish to acknowledge the use of the copyright photographs as follows: Camera Press: cover, title page and pages 40, 41 (3), 42, 43 (2), 44 and back cover; Tim Graham: pages 8 (top), 9 (top), 10 (2), 11, 12 (bottom), 13 (top), 14 (top and bottom left), 15 (2), 16 (2), 17 (2), 18 (3), 19 (top and bottom right), 20 (2), 22 (top), 23 (3), 24 (top), 25, 26 (2), 32 (2), 33 and 38/9 (bottom); Anwar Hussein: pages 4 (bottom right), 8 (bottom left), 19 (centre), 24 (bottom right), 36 (bottom right) and 39 (top); Rex Features: front endpaper and pages 4 (top and bottom left), 5 (2), 6, 7 (2), 19 (bottom left), 21 (3), 22 (bottom), 24 (bottom left) and 34 (top); Syndication International: pages 8/9 (bottom), 12 (top), 13 (bottom), 14 (bottom right), 27, 28 (2), 29 (2), 30 (2), 31 (2), 34 (bottom), 35 (2), 36 (top and bottom left), 37 (3) and 38 (left). Designed by Graham Marlow.

British Library Cataloguing in Publication Data

The Royal princes William & Henry. — (Famous people; v. 6)
 1. Henry, *Prince, grandson of Elizabeth II,*
 Queen of Great Britain — Portraits, caricatures,
 etc. — Juvenile literature.   2. William, *Prince,*
 grandson of Elizabeth II, Queen of Great Britain
 — Portraits, caricatures, etc. — Juvenile literature
 I. Daly, Audrey   II. Series
 941.085'092'2   DA591.A45H4

 ISBN 0-7214-0905-9

First Edition

© LADYBIRD BOOKS LTD MCMLXXXV

A 41-gun salute for a Royal Prince who is now second in line for the British throne

Crowds at the Palace

*A visitor for the newest member of the royal family –
his grandmother, Her Majesty Queen Elizabeth II*

*From the other
side of the
family:
Earl Spencer,
Prince William's
grandfather and
father of the
Princess of
Wales*

*and the
Honourable
Mrs Shand-Kydd,
Prince William's
grandmother,
and mother of
the Princess of
Wales*

7

The world's first view of baby William

The prince's birth certificate

Mother takes charge

Four generations at Prince William's christening. It took place in the Music Room at Buckingham Palace. The Queen Mother – the baby's great-grandmother – was 82 that same day: 4th August 1982

Happy in Kensington Palace, with his father, mother – and a favourite cuddly toy

Kensington Palace (shown above), is just one of the buildings that Prince William can call 'home'

Some of the furniture chosen for the new prince's nursery

William was just eighteen months old when he took his first 'photocall' in the garden at Kensington Palace

His mother and father went to great trouble to get the little boy to smile. "Who's that?" asked his mother, pointing at her husband

"Daddy!" said William, smiling at last

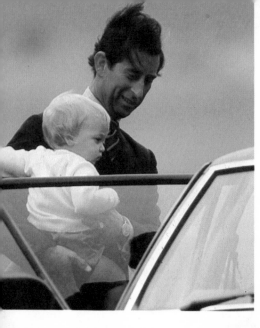

Some fathers leave the children to Mum. Not so Prince Charles — whenever he can, he likes to help. Here he is seen carrying Prince William after the plane landed at Aberdeen airport. The family was on its way to a favourite holiday home, Balmoral

At their Scottish
home of Balmoral
(shown above), the
royal family can
count on a little
more privacy than
usual. The lucky
snapshot on the
right however
shows Prince
William being
taken out by his
nanny, Barbara
Barnes, in
company with
his cousin
Zara Phillips and
her nanny

Nowadays travelling is something that royal princes start early — Prince William was the first royal baby to go on an official tour

Here he is seen (right) on arrival at Alice Springs, Australia, with his nanny, and (below) with his mother, also in Australia

Then on to New Zealand

A baby prince gets a great many toys, some very unusual. Some are really super – like the fire engine from Auckland Fire Service in New Zealand and the cuddly bear from Perth, Australia. The Paddington bear from student nurses at St Mary's Hospital, Paddington, London is traditional for all royal babies born there

A small violin for a small prince (above)

A 19th century rattle from the village of Tetbury, near Highgrove, home of the Prince of Wales and his family

A tiny piano from singer Barry Manilow (below left)

A model boat from Papua, New Guinea

Prince Charles was present when his son was born. He intends to be equally involved with every stage of his family's upbringing

Here he takes firm charge of William

On the other hand, when the little boy once decided to 'go it alone', up the steps of the plane, his father let him get on with it. He did make sure however that he was within reach to give a helping hand!

In the past royal children and their parents have never travelled in the same plane in case of accidents. So when Prince William flew to Aberdeen with his mother and father, it was yet another 'first' for the royal family

JUST
2
YEARS
OLD!

Prince William faced the cameras again on his second birthday, backed up by his mother and father. He was grave and a little unsure, but soon gained confidence. The Prince of Wales showed him how to kick a ball, and William took his time deciding what to do. Was the ball the wrong shape, perhaps? He might well prefer Rugby football in the future!

"Come on, Daddy, give me a push!" A request that doesn't really need putting into words as Prince Charles pops his son into a safe, solid-looking swing and does as he is asked.

Even in the most ordinary family, a toddler of two is usually the centre of attention.

And for a birthday prince, there's no end to the fun. ''Please may I look at that?'' Cameramen and television reporters were delighted to tell young William what he wanted to know

Trooping the Colour (a yearly ceremony in honour of the Queen's official birthday) — with an interested young prince watching from the balcony of Buckingham Palace. Nearly all small boys like soldiers and horses — and these are the best in the world. No wonder he is paying such attention to them!

Trooping the Colour goes on – and that's my grandmother down there

– and isn't that Daddy?

Daddy's back – good!

Mum is a very important person for any little boy. For Prince William, Mum is the Princess of Wales – beautiful, young and an acknowledged leader of fashion, with a style all her own

And then – a newcomer on the scene. Once more the happy crowds are kept at a discreet distance by the police as the Princess of Wales awaits the birth of her second baby. Then Prince Charles shakes hands with his well-wishers – it's another boy, Prince Henry, born on 15th September 1984

One of the first gifts for the new baby –

and flowers for his mother

Gun salutes and town criers
(shown right) are all part
of announcing the birth of a
royal baby. So too is the
announcement (below) on the
gates of Buckingham Palace.
Crowds always gather to find
out just what it says, even
though they know the news

Going to see
Mum – and
the new baby.
Prince Charles
takes William
into St Mary's
Hospital to
see his
mother for
the first time
since his
brother Henry
was born

A slightly bewildered little boy is led down the steps by his nanny, and then is strapped carefully into his safety seat to go home

Very little could be seen of the new prince when he left the hospital with his mother and father. He was well wrapped up against the damp weather

Prince Henry on show, in these first family portraits, taken by Lord Snowdon

The Princess of Wales once taught in a nursery school, and has a natural affection for small children. Along with Prince Charles, she is determined that their children should share a happy family life

The Christening of Prince Henry
on 21st December 1984

43